50 States of Cats

by Ted Meyer

5500 Hollywood Blvd. 3rd Floor •Los Angeles, California 90028
twitter.com/rothcopress
facebook.com/rothcopress
www.RothcoPress.com

First Edition: September 2014

Rothco Press name and logo are trademarks of Co-Conspiracy Entertainment.

The publisher is not responsible for websites (or their content) that are not owned by the publisher.

ISBN: 978-1-941519-24-0

For all my furry pals...

past and present

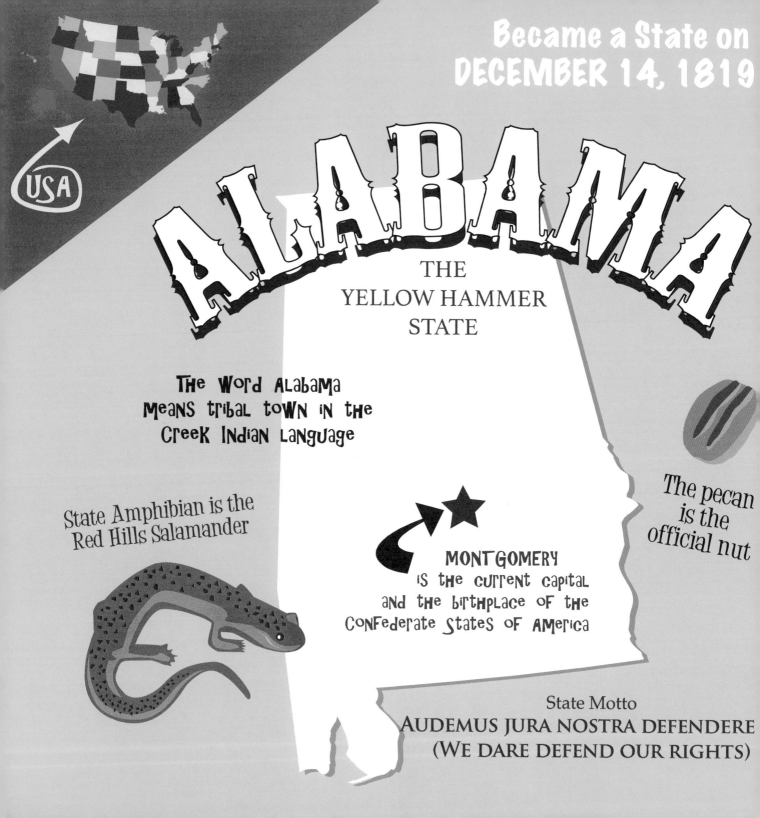

USA

Became a State on
JANUARY 3, 1959

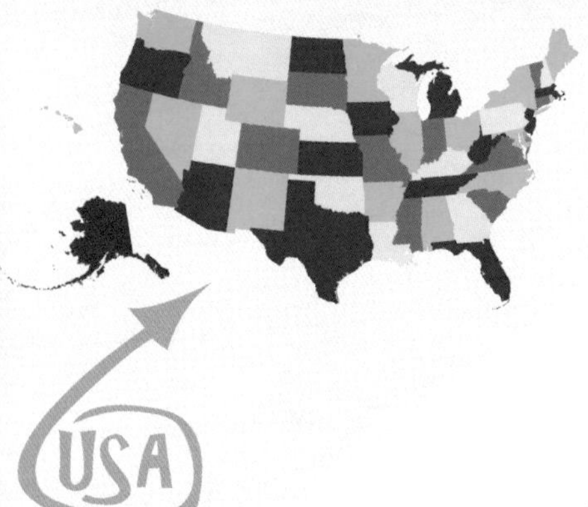

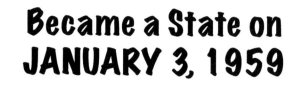

ALASKA

The Last Frontier

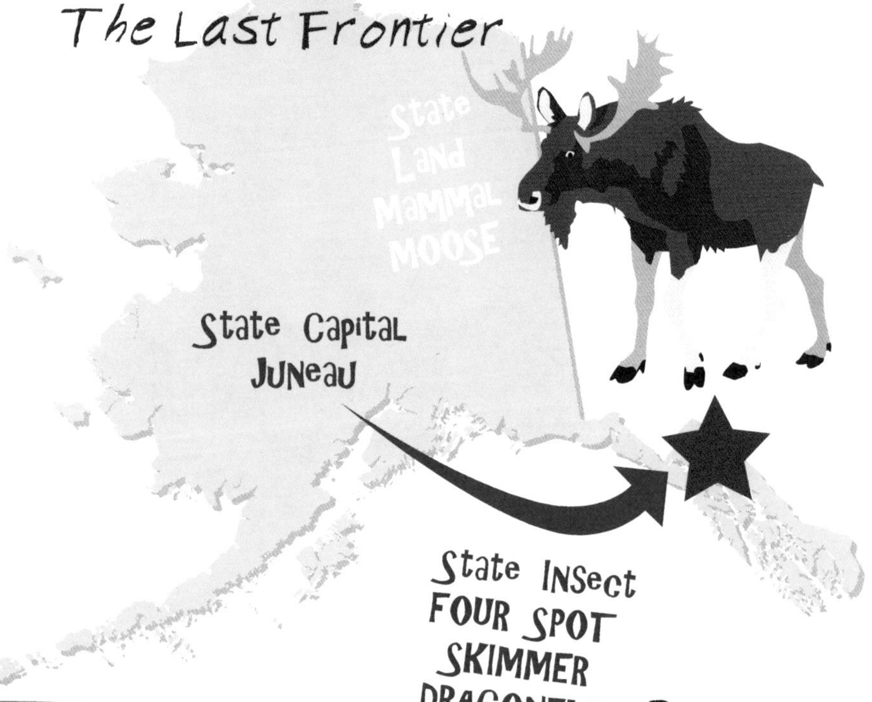

State Land Mammal MOOSE
State Capital JUNEAU

ALASKA HAS THE LONGEST COASTLINE IN THE U.S., 6640 MILES, GREATER THAN THAT OF ALL OTHER STATES COMBINED

State Insect
FOUR SPOT SKIMMER DRAGONFLY

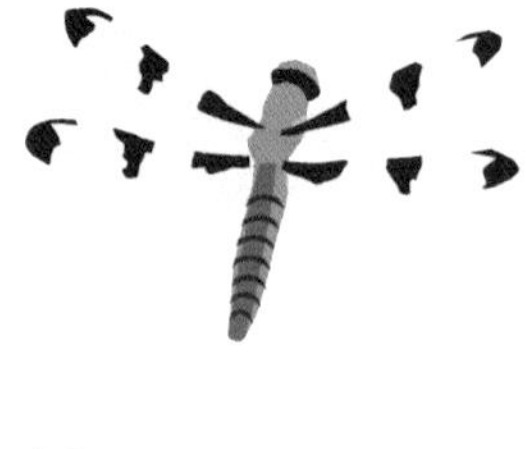

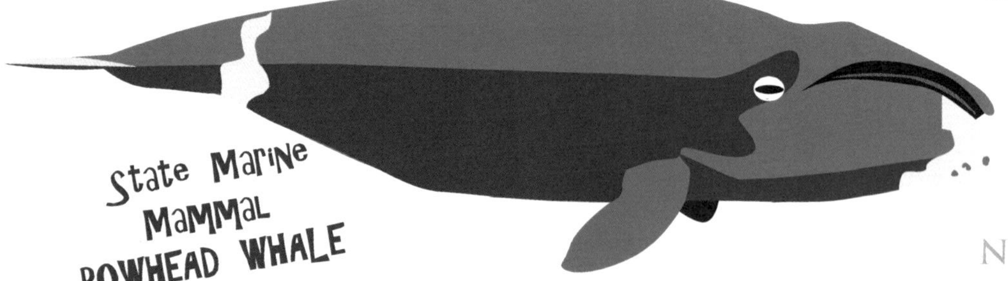

State Marine Mammal
BOWHEAD WHALE

State Motto
NORTH TO THE FUTURE

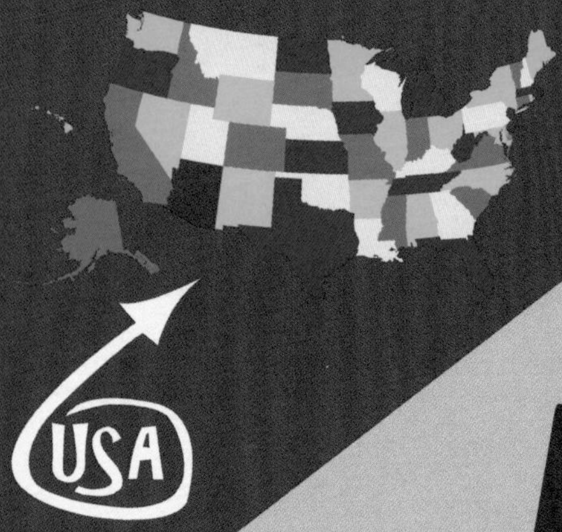

USA

ARIZONA
THE GRAND CANYON STATE

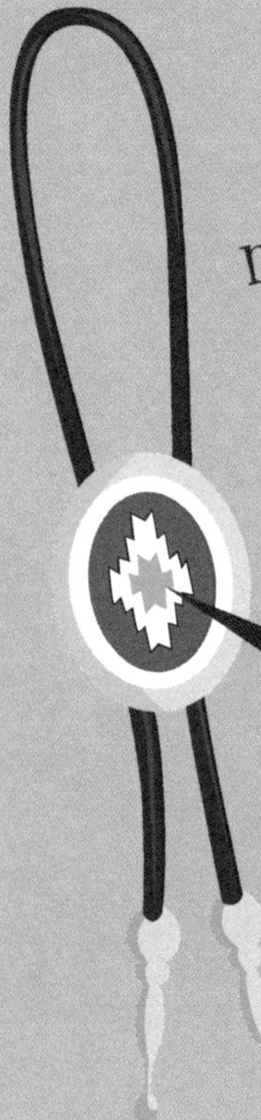

State
neckwear
is the
BOLO TIE

State
GeM is
TURQUOISE

State Capital
PHOENIX

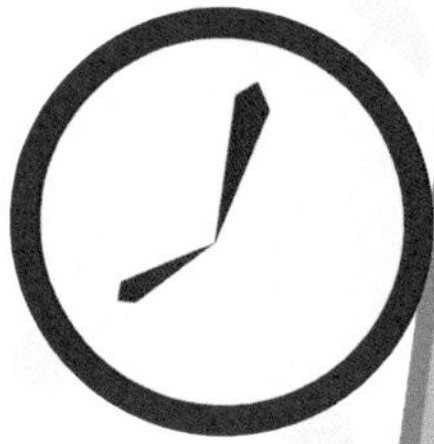

State Flower
SAGUARO CACTUS
FLOWER

ARIZONA
IS THE
ONLY State
iN THE
CONTINENTAL
U.S. that
doeSN't
FOLLOW
DayLIGHT
SaViNGS
TiME

State Motto
Ditat Deus
(God enriches)

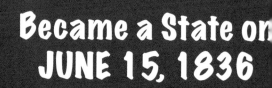

ARKANSAS
The Natural State

singers
Johnny Cash
& Janis Joplin
were born here

ARKANSAS HAS
THE ONLY active
diamond MiNE
iN THE U.S.

★ State Capital
LITTLE ROCK

President
Bill Clinton
was born here

State
INSTRUMENT
FIDDLE

State Motto
REGNAT POPULUS
(THE PEOPLE RULE)

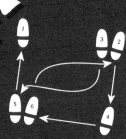

State Dance
SQUARE DANCE

California

The Golden State

State Mammal
GRIZZLY BEAR

A STAND OF 4000 YEAR OLD
BRISTLECONE PINES IN NORTHERN
CALIFORNIA ARE THE
WORLD'S OLDEST LIVING THINGS

CALIFONIA
GROWS MORE FOOD
THAN ANY OTHER STATE

State Capital
Sacramento

State reptile
DESERT
TORTOIS

State Fossil
SABERTOOTH
TIGER

State Marine Mammal
GRAY WHALE

PRESIDENT
RICHARD M. NIXON
WAS BORN HERE

State Motto
EUREKA
(I HAVE FOUND IT)

Became a State on
JANUARY 9, 1788

CONNECTICUT

The Constitution State

Connecticut comes from a Mohican/Algonquin Indian word "quonehtacut", which means "long tidal river"

State Capital
HARTFORD

President George Walker Bush Was born here

The Frisbee was invented here at YALE University

State Animal
SPERM WHALE

State Bird
ROBIN

Sculptor Alexander Calder had a home & Studio here

State Motto
**QUI TRANSTULIT SUSTINET
(HE WHO TRANSPLANTED SUSTAINS)**

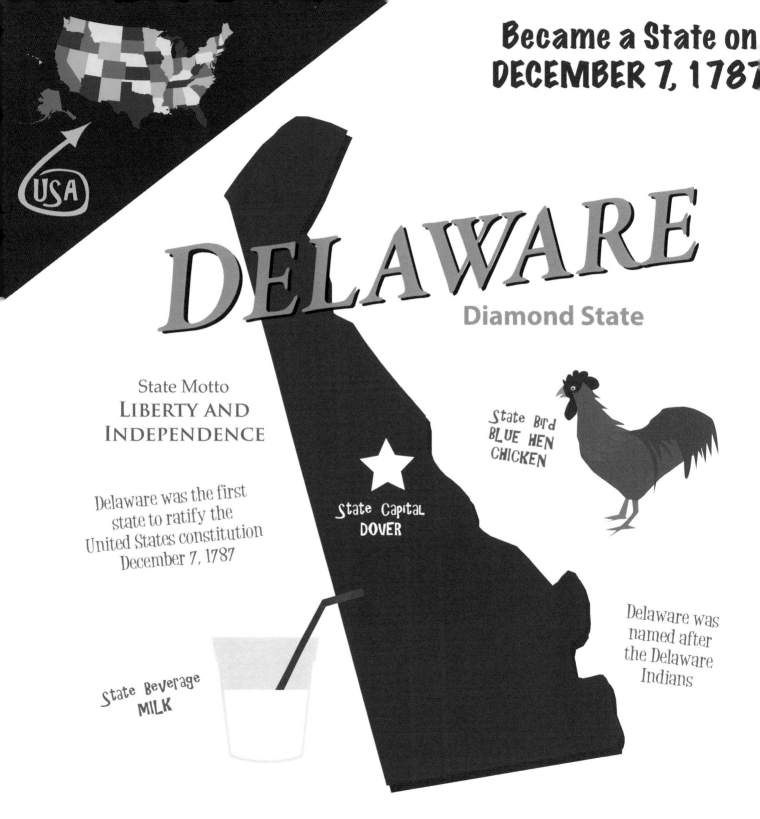

Became a State on
DECEMBER 7, 1787

DELAWARE

Diamond State

State Motto
LIBERTY AND INDEPENDENCE

Delaware was the first state to ratify the United States constitution December 7, 1787

State Bird
BLUE HEN CHICKEN

State Capital
DOVER

Delaware was named after the Delaware Indians

State Beverage
MILK

USA

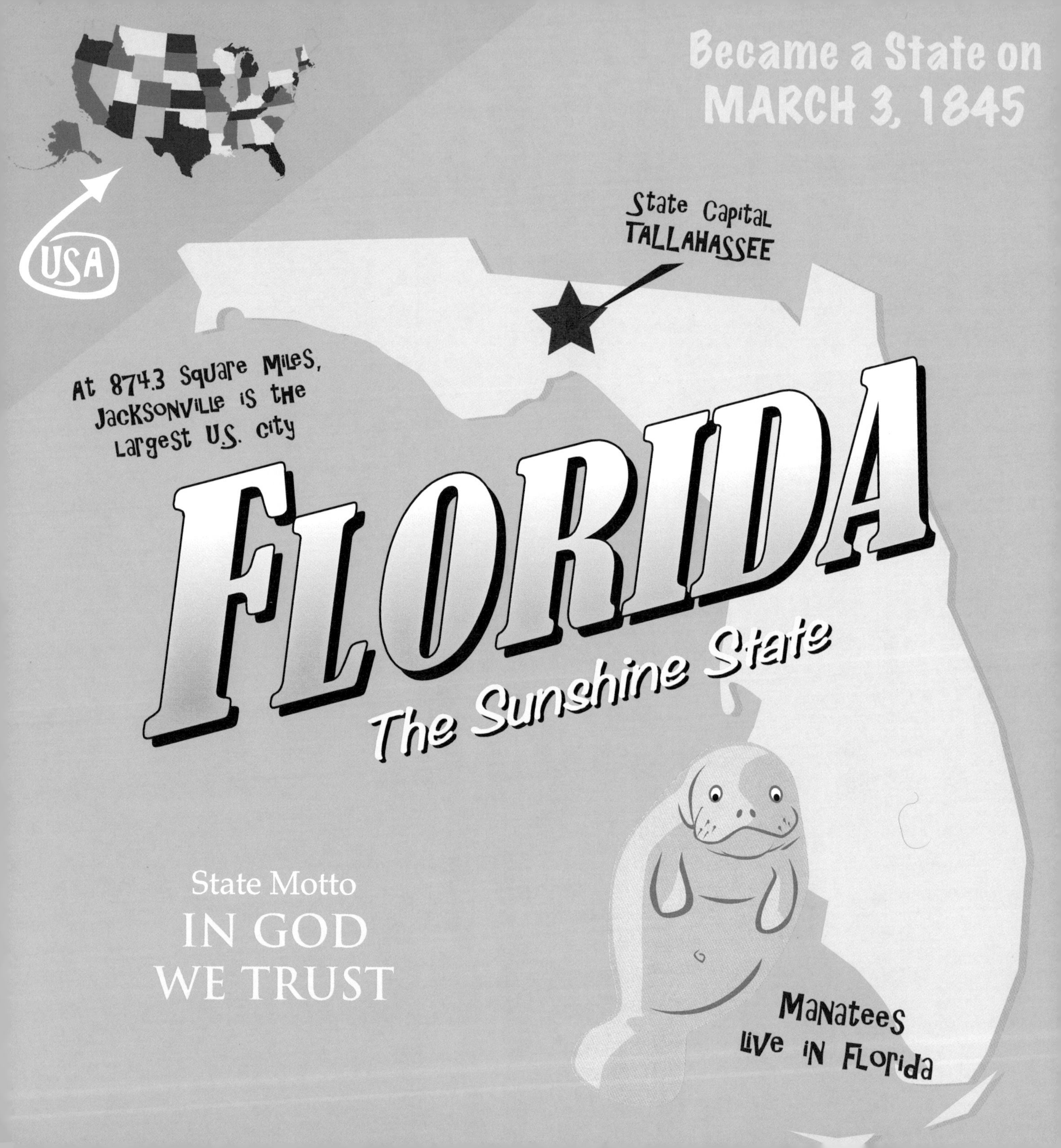

Became a State on
MARCH 3, 1845
USA
State Capital
TALLAHASSEE
At 874.3 Square Miles,
Jacksonville is the
Largest U.S. city
FLORIDA
The Sunshine State
State Motto
IN GOD
WE TRUST
Manatees
live in Florida

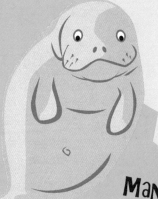

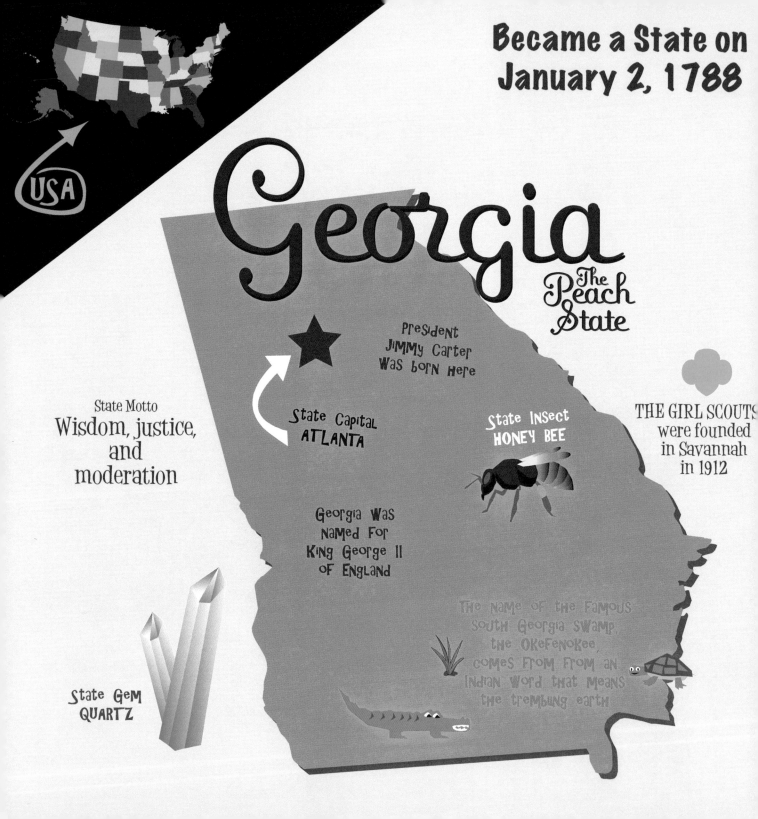

Became a State on
January 2, 1788

Georgia
The Peach State

President JiMMy Carter Was born here

State Motto
Wisdom, justice, and moderation

State Capital
ATLANTA

State INSect
HONEY BEE

THE GIRL SCOUTS were founded in Savannah in 1912

Georgia Was NaMed For KiNg George II oF ENgland

The NaMe oF the FaMous South Georgia SWaMp, the OkeFeNokee, coMes FroM FroM an INdian Word that MeaNs the treMblINg earth

State GeM
QUARTZ

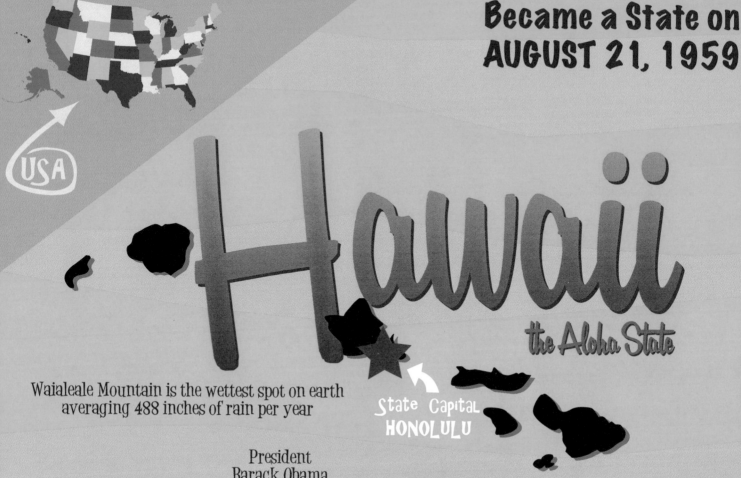

USA

Hawaii
the Aloha State

Waialeale Mountain is the wettest spot on earth averaging 488 inches of rain per year

State Capital
HONOLULU

President
Barack Obama
was born here

Hawaii is the only state
that grows coffee

State Motto:
Ua mau ke ea o ka aina i ka pono
(The life of the land is
perpetuated in righteousness)

State Mammal
MONK SEAL

State Flower
HIBISCUS

IDAHO
The Gem State

THE
AVERAGE AMERICAN
EATS ABOUT
124 POUNDS
OF POTATOES
PER YEAR

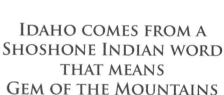

State Insect
MONARCH
BUTTERFLY

IDAHO COMES FROM A
SHOSHONE INDIAN WORD
THAT MEANS
GEM OF THE MOUNTAINS

State Capital
BOISE

State Gem
GARNET

State Bird
BLUEBIRD

State Motto
ESTO PERPETUA
(LET IT BE
PERPETUAL)

ILLINOIS

Prairie State

State Motto
State sovereignty, National Union

Lincoln was fond of pets, and owned horses, cats, dogs and a turkey

PRESIDENT RONALD REAGAN was born in ILLINOIS

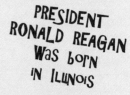

State bird
CARDINAL

State Capital
SPRINGFIELD

State Mammal
WHITE-TAILED DEER

ILLINOIS Was the First State to ratify the 13TH AMENDMENT to the Constitution abolishing Slavery in 1865

LINCOLN & OBAMA both Lived Here

USA

Indiana
Hoosier State

Indiana means
Land of
the Indians

The first professional
baseball game was played
in Fort Wayne on
May 4, 1871

the Indy 500
race happens
in Indianapolis

State Capital
INDIANAPOLIS

State Bird
CARDINAL

JAMES DEAN
Was born February 8, 1941
in Marion

State Motto
The Crossroads
of America

Became a State on
DECEMBER 28, 1846

IOWA Hawkeye State

Total annual egg production is 14.5 billion

there are 20.6 million hogs in Iowa

State Motto
OUR LIBERTIES WE PRIZE AND OUR RIGHTS WE WILL MAINTAIN

State Capital
DES MOINES

Iowa produces 1.88 billion bushels of corn a year

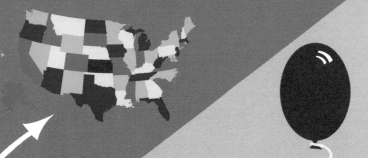

KANSAS

SUNFLOWER STATE

Dodge City is the
windiest city
in the United States

State Capital
TOPEKA

State Animal
BISON

State Motto
AD ASTRA PER ASPERA
(TO THE STARS
THROUGH DIFFICULTIES)

Helium was discovered in 1905
at the University of Kansas

USA

Kentucky

Bluegrass State

More than $6 billion worth
of gold is held in the
underground vaults of Fort Knox

★

State Capital
FRANKFORT

State Wild Animal
GRAY SQUIRREL

Thomas Edison introduced his
incandescent light bulb at the
Southern Exposition in 1883

State Bird
CARDINAL

State Motto
UNITED WE STAND,
DIVIDED WE FALL

State Fish
KENTUCKY BASS

Bluegrass is not actually blue, it is green,
but in the spring time bluegrass produces
bluish purple buds that give it a blue color

Became a State on
JANUARY 29, 1861

USA

Louisiana

The Pelican State

State Crustacean
CRAWFISH

State Bird
**EASTERN BROWN
PELICAN**

State Capital
BATON ROUGE

State
Beverage
MILK

State Mammal
**LOUISIANA
BLACK BEAR**

Louisiana has parishes instead
of counties because they
were originally Spanish church units

State Motto
**UNION, JUSTICE,
CONFIDENCE**

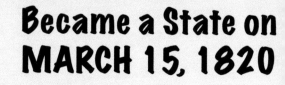

USA

Maine
Pine Tree State

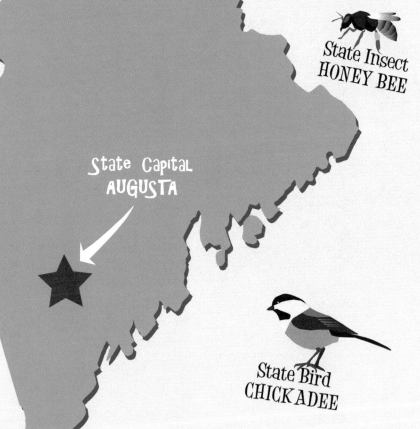

Maine produces 99% of all the blueberries in the country

State Insect
HONEY BEE

State Capital
AUGUSTA

Maine is so big it covers as many square miles as the other five New England states combined

State Motto
DIRIGO
(I DIRECT)

State Bird
CHICKADEE

Maryland

Became a State on APRIL 28, 1788

USA

Old Line State & Free State

State Capital
ANNAPOLIS

THE State Crustacean IS THE MARYLAND BLUE CRAB

State Motto
FATTI MASCHII, PAROLE FEMINE
(MANLY DEEDS, WOMANLY WORDS)

THE Ouija board was created IN BALTIMORE IN 1892

Became a State on
FEBRUARY. 6, 1788

MASSACHUSETTS

THE BAY STATE

State Capital
BOSTON

Paul Revere did his
midnight ride here

The Fig Newton
is named after
Newton, Massachusetts

State Bird
CHICKADEE

The first World Series in 1903
pitted the Boston Americans
(became the Red Sox in 1908)
against the Pittsburg Pirates
(no H at the end of Pittsburgh back then)

State Motto
ENSE PETIT PLACIDAM SUB
LIBERTATE QUIETEM IN LATIN
(BY THE SWORD WE SEEK PEACE,
BUT PEACE ONLY UNDER LIBERTY)

MICHIGAN

WOLVERINE STATE

Michigan is from an
Algonquian Chippewa
Indian word
"Meicigama" that
means Big Lake

Although
Michigan is nick named
the Wolverine State
there are no longer
any wolverines in
Michigan

Henry Ford
Made cars
here

State
Bird
ROBIN

State Capital
LANSING

State Motto
SI QUAERIS PENINSULAM
AMOENAM CIRCUMSPICE
(IF YOU SEEK A PLEASANT
PENINSULA, LOOK ABOUT YOU)

USA

USA

Minnesota

The Gopher State • North Star State • Land of 10,000 Lakes

PAUL BUNYAN AND BABE THE BLUE OX
ARE SAID TO BE FROM
BEMIDJI, MINNESOTA

State FISH
WALLEYE

State INSECT
MONARCH
BUTTERFLY

State Capital
ST. PAUL

State BIrd
COMMON LOON

State MUFFIN
BLUEBERRY

State Motto
L'ÉTOILE DU NORD
(THE STAR OF THE NORTH)

Mississippi
Magnolia State

USA

Elvis Presley
was born in
Tupelo, on
January 8, 1935

State
Bird
MOCKINGBIRD

President
Teddy Roosevelt
refused to shoot
a bear here ...
that's how the
teddy bear
got its name

State Capital
JACKSON

State
Water Mammal
**BOTTLENOSED
DOLPHIN**

State Motto
**VIRTUTE ET ARMIS
(BY VALOR AND ARMS)**

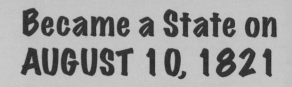

USA

Missouri

The Show Me State

State FiSH
PADDLEFISH

Samuel Clemens
(better known by his
pen name Mark Twain)
was born here

Missouri was named for
an Algonquian Indian
word that means
river of the big canoes

State Bird
MISSOURI BLUEBIRD

State Capital
JEFFERSON CITY

State ANiMAL
MISSOURI MULE

State Motto
**SALUS POPULI SUPREMA LEX ESTO
(THE WELFARE OF THE PEOPLE
SHALL BE THE SUPREME LAW)**

President
Harry S. Truman
was born here

USA

MONTANA
Big Sky Country

State Motto
SALUS POPULI SUPREMA LEX ESTO
(THE WELFARE OF THE PEOPLE
SHALL BE THE SUPREME LAW)

**State Bird
MEADOWLARK**

**State Animal
GRIZZLY BEAR**

**State Capital
HELENA**

No state has as
many different species
of mammals as Montana

**State Tree
PONDEROSA PINE**

USA

NEBRASKA

Cornhusker State

State Fossil
MAMMOTH

Nebraska ranks #2
in the number of cattle
(behind Texas)

State Soft Drink
KOOL-AID
Developed in Hastings,
Nebraska in 1927

President
Gerald Ford
was born here

State Capital
LINCOLN

State Motto
**Equality
before
the law**

1.55 billion
bushels of corn
a year

Nebraska is the birthplace of
the Reuben Sandwich and Spam

USA

Became a State on
OCTOBER 31, 1864

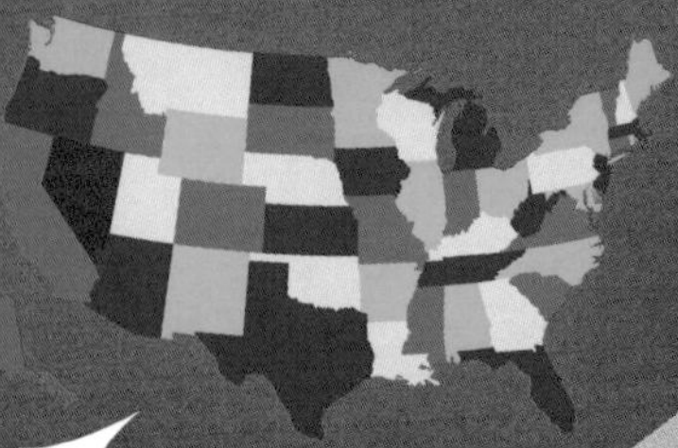

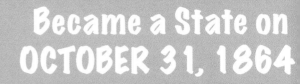

NEVADA

Silver State & Sagebrush State

State Capital
CARSON CITY

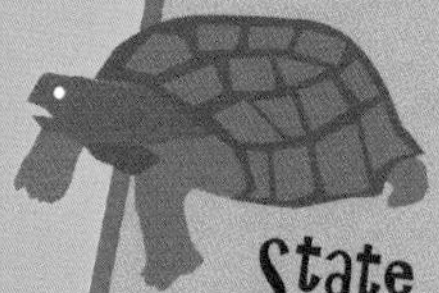

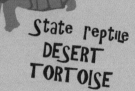

State reptile
DESERT TORTOISE

State Animal
BIG HORNED SHEEP

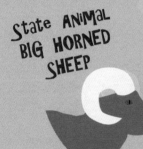

Nevada is the largest gold-producing state in the nation

State Motto
All for Our Country

Nevada is from the Spanish word meaning snowcapped

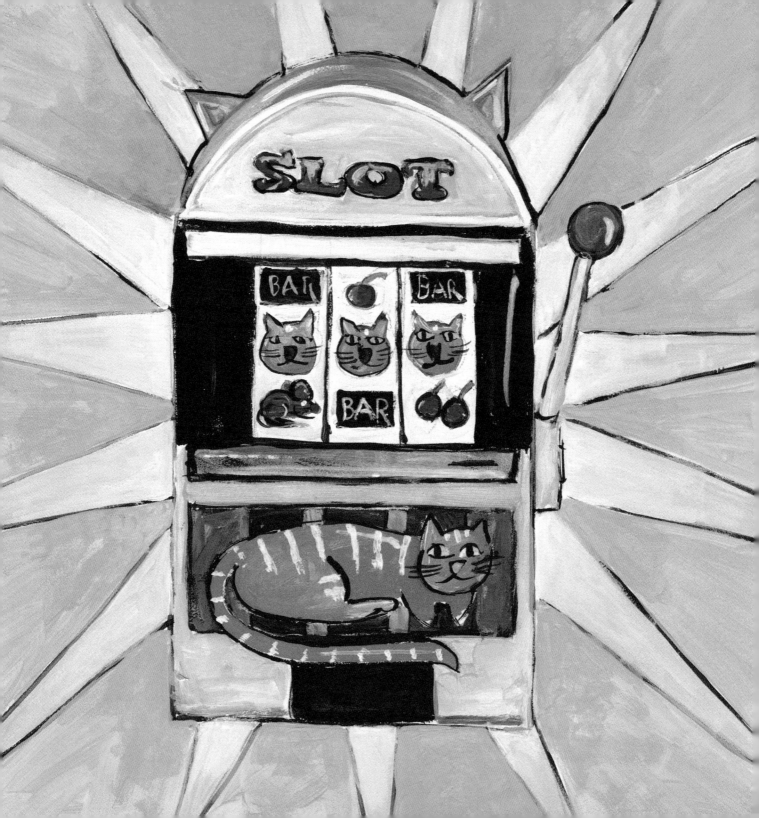

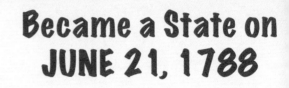

Became a State on JUNE 21, 1788

New Hampshire

GRANITE STATE

USA

State butterfly
KARNER BLUE BUTTERFLY

State Bird
PURPLE FINCH

New Hampshire was the first colony to declare independence from England

President Franklin Pierce was born in Hillsborough

State Capital
CONCORD

New Hampshire always hosts the first presidential primaries

State Motto
Live Free or Die

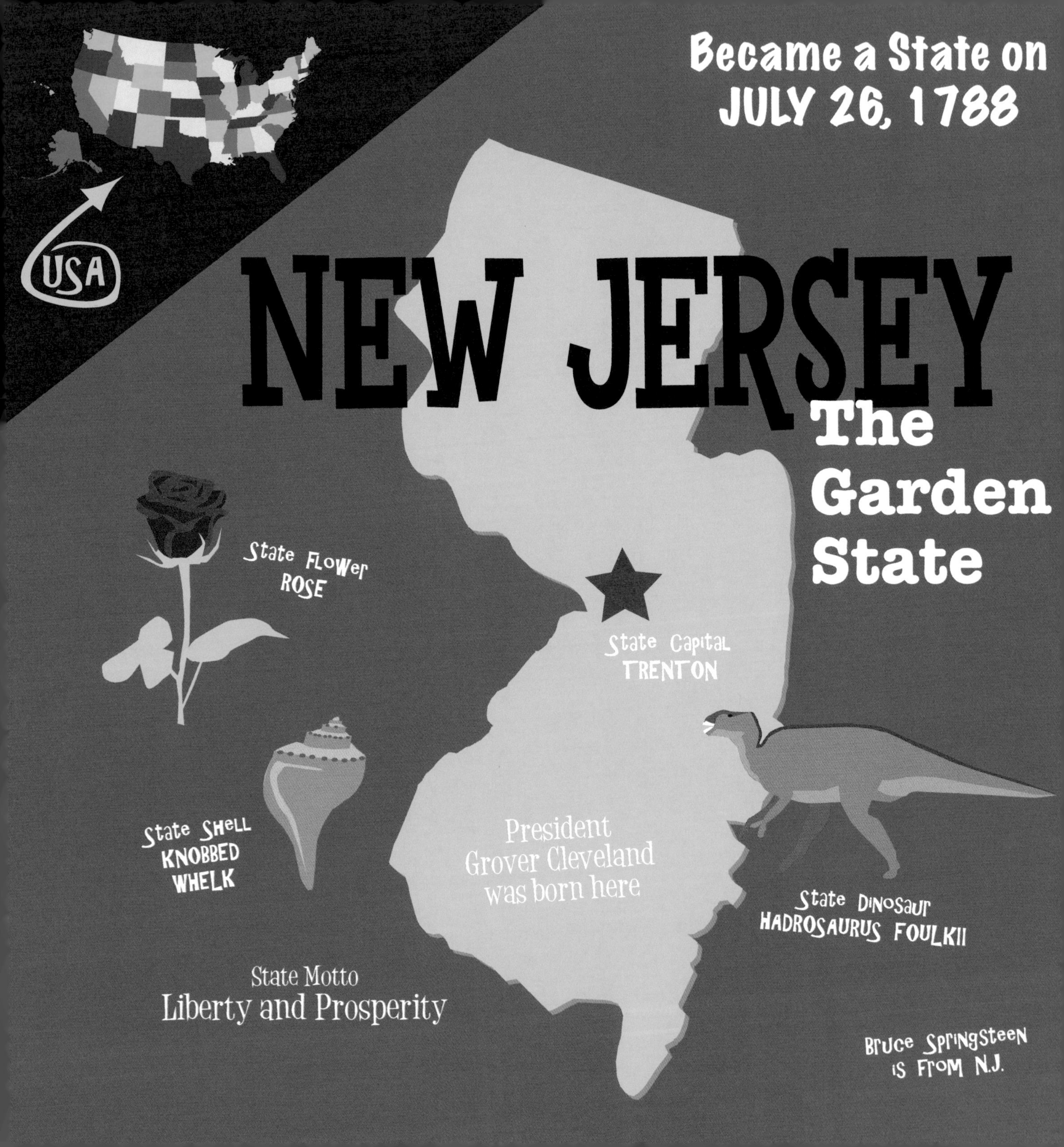

USA
Became a State on
JULY 26, 1788
NEW JERSEY
The Garden State
State Flower
ROSE
State Capital
TRENTON
State Shell
KNOBBED WHELK
President Grover Cleveland was born here
State Dinosaur
HADROSAURUS FOULKII
State Motto
Liberty and Prosperity
Bruce Springsteen is from N.J.

USA

NEW MEXICO

The Land of Enchantment

Santa Fe is the highest capital city in the United States at 7000 feet above sea level

State Capital
SANTA Fe

State BIRD
ROAD
RUNNER

State DiNOSAUR
COELOPHYSIS

The Navajo reservation covers 14 million Acres

State Motto
Crescit eundo
(It grows
as it goes)

It is said that
Aliens crash landed in
Roswell N.M. in 1947

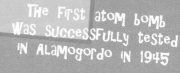

The First atom bomb
Was successfully tested
in Alamogordo in 1945

Became a State on
JULY 26, 1788

NEW YORK
The Empire State

Presidents
Martin Van Buren
Millard Fillmore
Theodore Roosevelt
and
Franklin Delano Roosevelt
were all born in N.Y.

State ANiMaL
BEAVER

State Capital
ALBANY

State Motto
**Excelsior
(Ever Upward)**

State Fruit
APPLE

State Insect
9 SPOTTED LADY BUG

USA

North Carolinia

Old North State

State Vegetable
SWEET POTATO

In 1903 the
Wright Brothers made
the first successful
powered flight
near Kitty Hawk

State Capital
RALEIGH

State bird
CARDINAL

State Motto
**Esse Quam Videri
(To Be Rather
Than to Seem)**

First State in the Nation
to establish a State
MUSEUM of art

Presidents
James K. Polk
& Andrew Johnson
were born here

USA

North Dakota

Peace Garden State

State Bird
MEADOWLARK

North Dakota grows
More SUNFLOWers
than any other state

State Flower
WILD PRAIRIE ROSE

State Capital
BISMARK

Dakota is a Sioux
word meaning
friends or allies

State Motto
Liberty and union,
now and forever,
one and inseparable

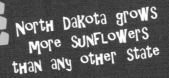

The Dakota Dinosaur Museum
in Dickinson Houses
twelve Full Scale
dinosaurs and a
complete REAL
Triceratops and
Edmontosaurus

OKLAHOMA
Sooner State

State Bird
Wild Turkey

State Furbearer
RACCOON

State Capital
OKLAHOMA
CITY

State Animal
BUFFALO

The National Cowboy
Hall of Fame
is located in Oklahoma City

OKLAHOMA comes from
from the Choctaw Indian
words "okla" meaning
people and "humma"
meaning red

State Motto
Labor omnia vincit
(Labor Conquers All Things)

OREGON
Beaver State

State Animal
AMERICAN BEAVER

State Capital
SALEM

State Fish
CHINOOK SALMON

Settlers road
the Oregon Trail
to the Oregon Territory
to get free farm land

The Oregon Trail
covered 6 states
starting in Missouri

State Motto
**She Flies With
Her Own Wings**

State Nut
HAZELNUT

State Mushroom
**PACIFIC GOLDEN
CHANTERELLE**

**Became a State on
DECEMBER 12, 1787**

Pennsylvania
Keystone State

State Motto
**Virtue, Liberty,
and Independence**

PUNXSUTAWNEY PHIL,
tHE GROUNDHOG,
LiVES HERE

President
James Buchanan
was born here

State Capital
HARRISBURG

THE
LIBERTY
BELL
iS HERE

State Dog
GREAT DANE

State INSECTS
LADY BUG &
FIREFLY

Rhode Island
THE OCEAN STATE

State Motto
Hope

State Capital
PROVIDENCE

State Flower
VIOLETS

State Bird
RHODE ISLAND RED

The Tennis
Hall of Fame is in
Rhode Island

Rhode Island is
the smallest state,
just 1214 square miles

Rhode Island comes from
"Rood Eylandt" meaning
Red Island in Dutch

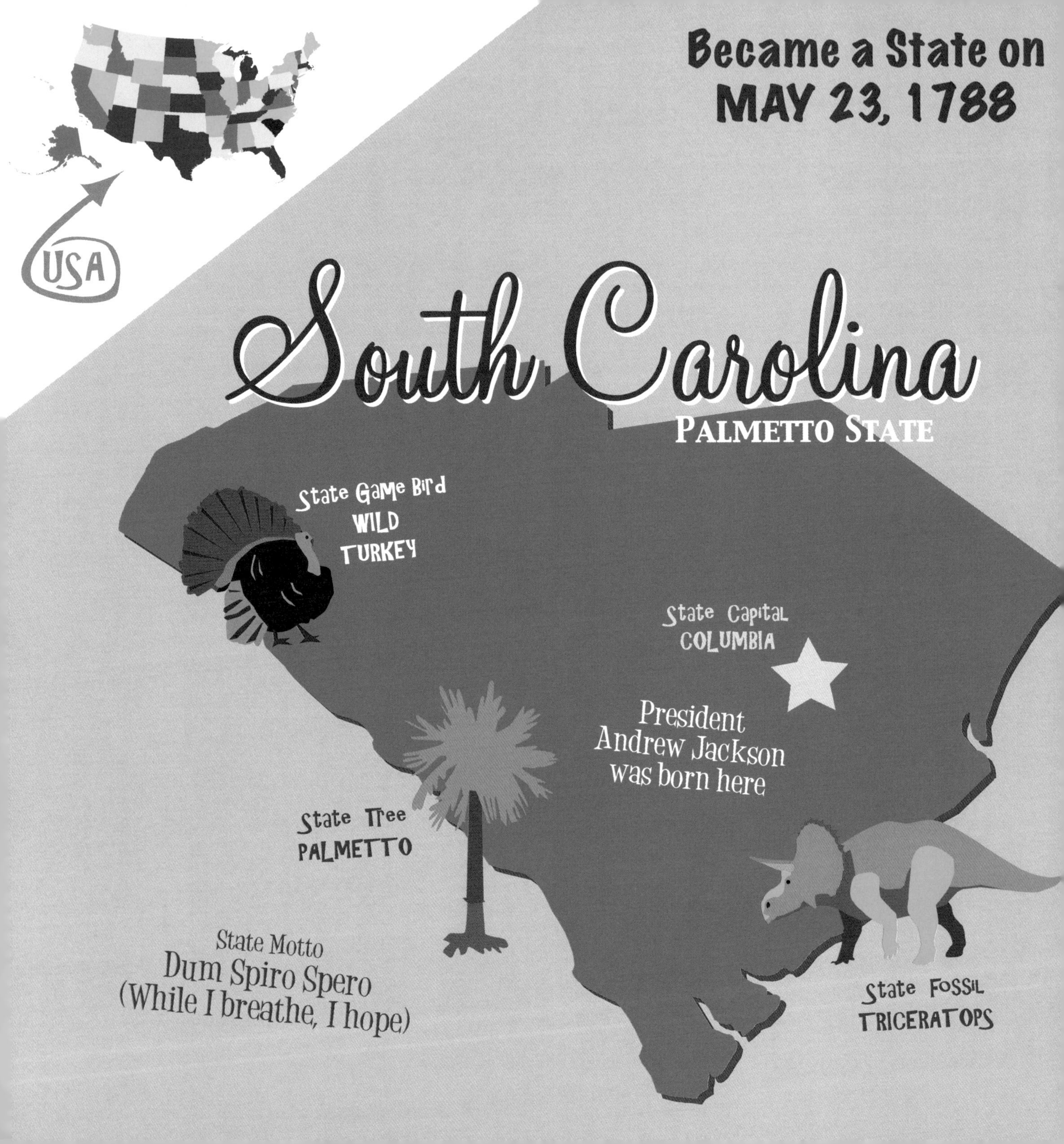

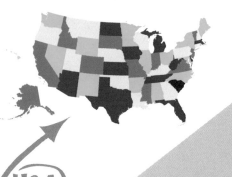

USA
Became a State on
MAY 23, 1788
South Carolina
PALMETTO STATE
State Game Bird
WILD
TURKEY
State Capital
COLUMBIA
President
Andrew Jackson
was born here
State Tree
PALMETTO
State Motto
Dum Spiro Spero
(While I breathe, I hope)
State Fossil
TRICERATOPS

South Dakota

Mount Rushmore State

State Capital
PIERRE

State Insect
HONEY BEE

State Animal
COYOTE

The faces of George Washington,
Thomas Jefferson, Theodore Roosevelt,
and Abraham Lincoln
are sculpted into Mount Rushmore

State Motto
Under God
the people rule

State Fossil
TRICERATOPS

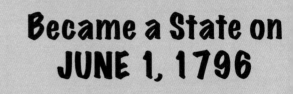

USA

Tennessee
The Volunteer State

State Commercial Fish
CHANNEL CATFISH

Davie Crocket
was born in
Limestone

State Capitol
NASHVILLE

ELVIS lived
IN MEMPHIS

State Game Bird
BOBWHITE QUAIL

The name Tennessee
comes from a Cherokee village
that was named "Tanasie"

State Motto
Agriculture and Commerce

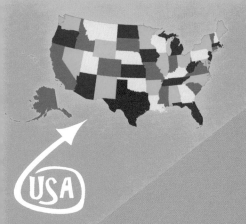

USA

Texas was once it's OWN NATION

State Bird
MOCKINGBIRD

The HAMBURGER was invented in Arlington in 1906

Texas
The Lone Star State

State Motto
Friendship

Presidents
Dwight D. Eisenhower
&
Lyndon B. Johnson
were born
here

State Capital
AUSTIN

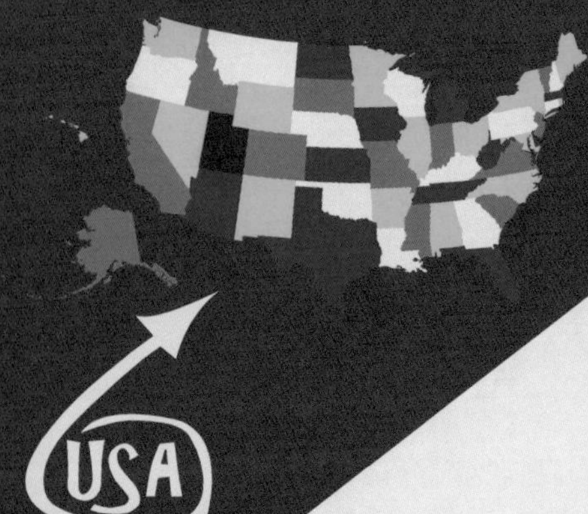

USA

UTAH
Beehive State

State Capital
SALT LAKE CITY

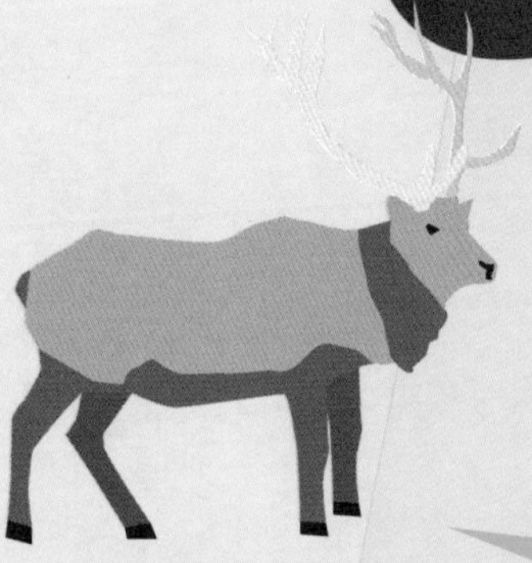

State ANIMAL
ROCKY MOUNTAIN
ELK

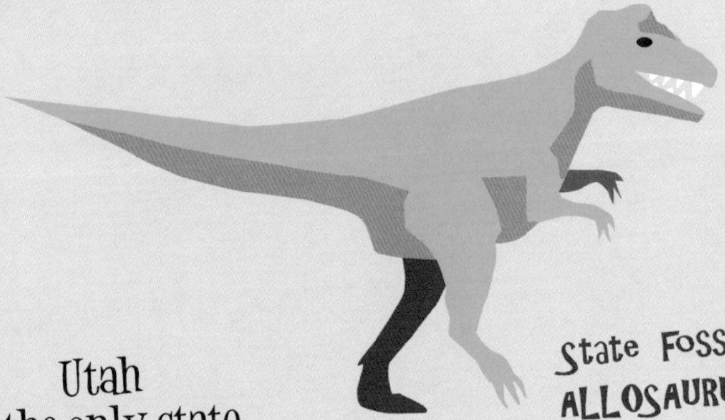

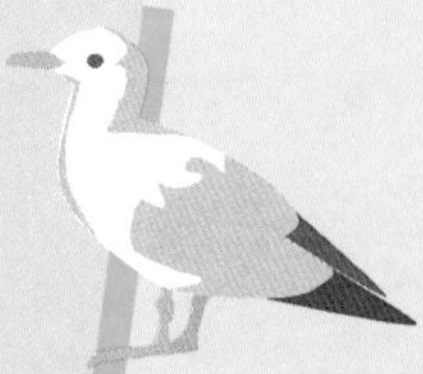

State Bird
SEAGULL

State FOSSIL
ALLOSAURUS

Utah
is the only state
with a three
word capital city

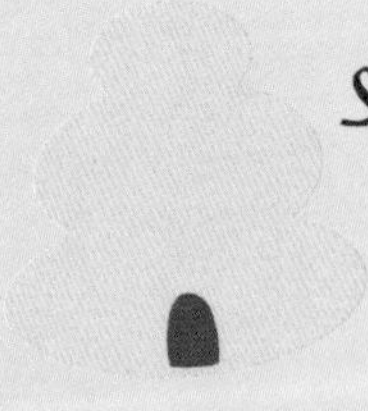

State SYMBOL
BEEHIVE

State Motto
Industry

The Great Salt Lake
covers 2100 square miles

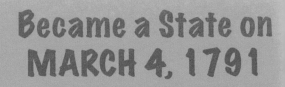

USA

Vermont

Green Mountain State

State Capital
MONTPELIER

State ANiMaL
MORGAN HORSE

Presidents
Chester Alan Arthur
&
Calvin Coolidge
were born here

Vermont is the
largest producer
of Maple Syrup
in the
United States

State AMPHibiaN
**NORTHERN
LEOPARD FROG**

State FLoWer
RED CLOVER

Maple syrup is produced
from the sap collected from
the Sugar Maple tree

State Motto
Freedom and Unity

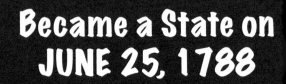

USA

Virginia
Old Dominion

State Capital
RICHMOND

Virgina is home
to Thomas Jefferson's
Monticello Plantation

State SHELL
OYSTER

State FLOWER
DOGWOOD

State Motto
Sic Semper Tyrannis
(Thus Always to Tyrants)

Presidents
George Washington,
Thomas Jefferson,
James Madison,
William Henry Harrison,
John Tyler,
Zachary Taylor
&
Woodrow Wilson
were born here

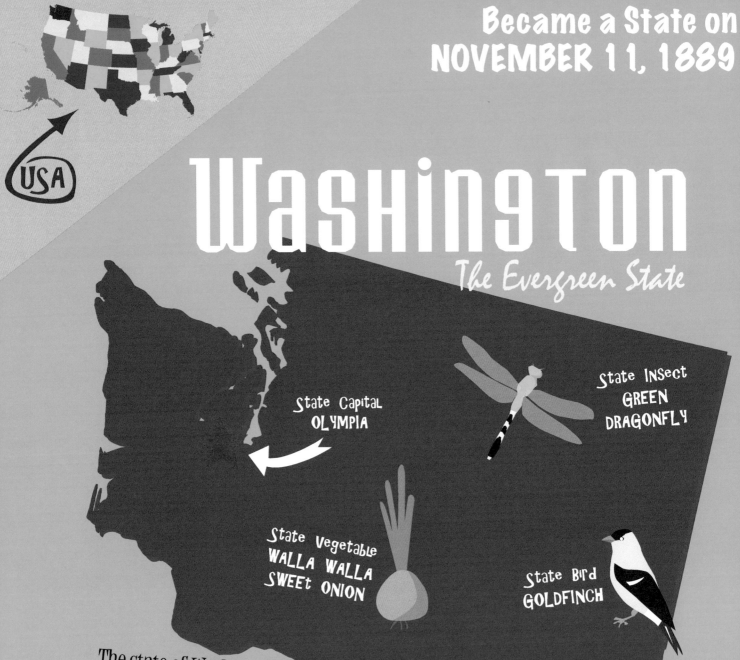

WEST VIRGINIA
Mountain State

West Virginia ranks #2 in coal production (behind Kentucky)

State ANIMAL
Black Bear

State Fruit
GOLDEN DELICIOUS APPLE

State Tree
SUGAR MAPLE

State Insect
MONARCH BUTTERFLY

State Capital
CHARLESTON

State Motto
Montani semper liberi
(Mountaineers are always free)

Became a State on JUNE 20, 1863

USA

WISCONSIN
Badger State

State ANIMAL
BADGER

State Symbol of Peace
MORNING DOVE

State Grain
CORN

Wisconsin is
number 1 in
milk production

State DOMESTIC ANIMAL
DAIRY COW

State Capital
MADISON

State Motto
Forward

WYOMING

Equality State

State Flower
INDIAN
PAINTBRUSH

State Fish
CUTTHROAT TROUT

State Animal
BUFFALO

the Artist
Jackson Pollock
was born here

State Gem
JADE

State Capital
CHEYENNE

State Reptile
HORNED LIZARD

State Motto
Equal Rights

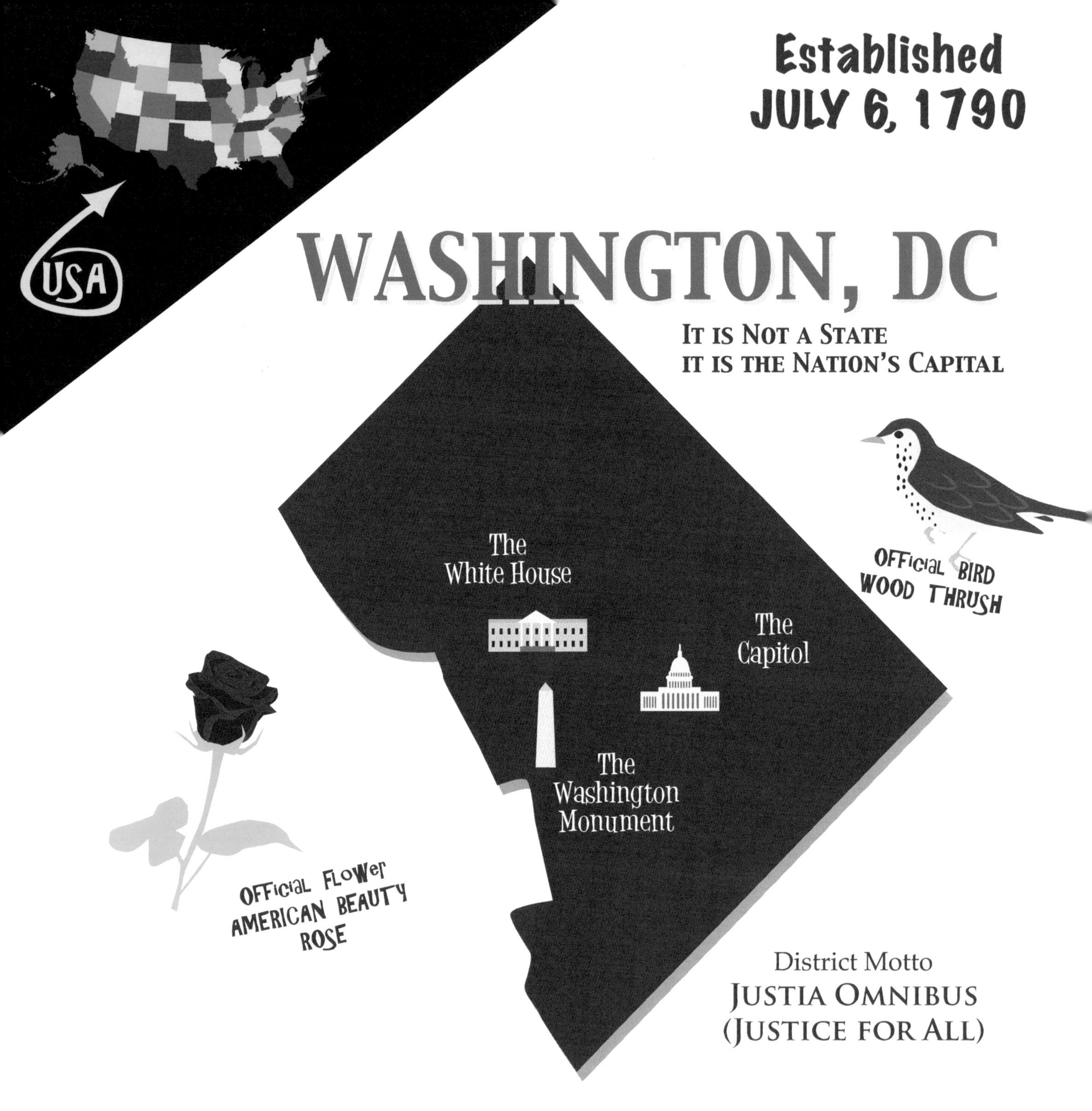

Established
JULY 6, 1790

WASHINGTON, DC

IT IS NOT A STATE
IT IS THE NATION'S CAPITAL

OFFiciaL BIRD
WOOD THRUSH

The
White House

The
Capitol

The
Washington
Monument

OFFiciaL FLOWer
AMERICAN BEAUTY
ROSE

District Motto
JUSTIA OMNIBUS
(JUSTICE FOR ALL)

Made in the USA
Charleston, SC
14 October 2014